Mike Barker

OCEAN THE MOST WONDERFUL

© Copyright 2021 - All rights reserved.

You may not reproduce, duplicate or send the contents of this book without direct written permission from the author. You cannot hereby despite any circumstance blame the publisher or hold him or her to legal responsibility for any reparation, compensations, or monetary forfeiture owing to the information included herein, either in a direct or an indirect way.

Legal Notice: This book has copyright protection. You can use the book for personal purpose. You should not sell, use, alter, distribute, quote, take excerpts or paraphrase in part or whole the material contained in this book without obtaining the permission of the author first.

Disclaimer Notice: You must take note that the information in this document is for casual reading and entertainment purposes only.

We have made every attempt to provide accurate, up to date and reliable information. We do not express or imply guarantees of any kind. The persons who read admit that the writer is not occupied in giving legal, financial, medical or other advice. We put this book content by sourcing various places.

Please consult a licensed professional before you try any techniques shown in this book. By going through this document, the book lover comes to an agreement that under no situation is the author accountable for any forfeiture, direct or indirect, which they may incur because of the use of material contained in this document, including, but not limited to, — errors, omissions, or inaccuraci

WELCOME TO THE OCEAN

OCEAN

An Ocean is a very huge body covered of salt water. It presents 70% of Earth's surface. There is only one world ocean, it is divided into five main areas with no borders. Smaller parts of the ocean are called seas.

ATLANTIC

Atlantic Ocean is the second largest of Earth's oceans. Most of Earth rivers water flow into the Atlantic. Its S-shaped basin extending longitudinally between Europe and Africa to the east, and the Americas to the west

PACIFIC

Pacific Ocean is the largest of Earth's oceans. Its surface is more than all the dry lands together. It is bounded by the continents of Asia and Australia in the west and the Americas in the east.

ARCTIC

Arctic Ocean is the world smallest and shallowest ocean. It is also known by being the coldest. than all the dry lands together. It occupies the most northern region of Earth.

INDIAN

Indian Ocean is the third largest of Earth's oceans. It was sailed by traders to exchange goods between India, Africa, and Arabia. It is bounded by Asia to the north, Africa to the west and Australia to the east

SOUTHERN

The Southern Ocean is also known as the Antarctic Ocean because it surrounds Antarctica.

OCEAN MOST WONDERFUL ANIMALS

My
Name
Is
CRAB

CRAB

I am decapod, which means I am ten-footed. I live in all the world's oceans, in fresh water, and on land. There are over 4500 species of me.

My

Name

Is

SHARK

SHARK

I don't have any bone in my body.
I live for about 25 years.
You might know me as human-killer
but I only attack if I am scared.

OCTOPUS

I have three hearts.
I have very good eyesight and
an excellent sense of touch.
I am invertebrate,
which means I have no backbones.

STARFISH

I can only live in warm water.
I am invertebrate too.
I have five arms.
Unlike you, I don't have blood.

My
Name
Is
OYSTER

OYSTER

I am edible. I like to eat algae, which is a type of plant material that lives in the water.
I have shells that are usually shaped like ovals or pears

DOLPHIN

I am a marine mammal.
I breathe through a blowhole on the top of my head.
I am carnivore, I eat mostly fish and squid. I m the most intelligent animal in the ocean.

SEA TURTLE

I can hold my breath for 30 minutes. I can't live on the Arctic Ocean because it's too cold there. eat all kinds of food including sea grass, seaweed, crabs, jellyfish, and shrimp

My
Name
Is
SEAL

SEAL

I am carnivorous mammal.
I usually feeds on fish,
squid, shellfish, crustaceans
or sea birds.
i can sleep underwater.

SEA HORSE

I am a tiny fis. They call me Sea horse cause my head looks like a tiny horse.
I am carnivore too.

Thank you. We hope you engjoyedour
book.
As a small family company, your feedback is very importantto us.
Pleaselet us know how you like our book at:
sellpublish@gmail.com

www.ingramcontent.com/pod-product-compliance
Lightning Source LLC
Chambersburg PA
CBHW051302110526
44589CB00025B/2912